Repentance

*What It Is, What It Isn't,
and How To Do It*

RICK RENNER

20 19 18 17   10 9 8 7 6 5 4 3 2 1

Repentance:
What It Is, What It Isn't, and How To Do It
ISBN: 978-1-68031-200-3

Copyright © 2017 by Rick Renner
8316 E. 73rd St.
Tulsa, OK 74133

Published by Harrison House Publishers
Tulsa, OK 74145
www.harrisonhouse.com

Editorial Consultant: Cynthia D. Hansen
Text Design: Lisa Simpson,
    www.SimpsonProductions.net
Cover: Debbie Pullman, Zoe Life Creative Media
    Design@ZoeLifeCreative.com, www.ZoeLifeCreative.com

Therefore leaving the principles
of the doctrines of Christ,
let us go unto perfection; not laying again
the foundation of repentance
from dead works,
and of faith toward God, of the doctrine
of baptisms, and of laying on of hands,
and of resurrection of the dead,
and of eternal judgment.

— Hebrews 6:1,2

truly repent and why repentance is
tely crucial ingredient of your walk
. I have taken great care to ensure that
ect of this discussion is rooted firmly
ord of God. As you study the truths
1 in these pages, I believe they will
be a powerful asset to enhance your
growth and deepen your intimacy
Lord. That is my prayer.

Rick Renner

CONTENTS

INTR(

In recent yea
teach on the subje
eled and ministe
globe. As a result,
a large number of
no knowledge of
why it's so founda
Christian walk.

Many believer
tance with remorse
repentance is little
out-of-jail-free card
fault, ask for forgi
back into the same
see, *personal change*
remorse, regret, and
of repentance.

The purpose of
with a comprehensi

means t
an abso
with Go
every as
in the V
containe
prove to
spiritua
with the

1

WHAT *IS* REPENTANCE?

What does it actually mean to "repent"?

In a recent national survey, churchgoers were asked to articulate what the word "repentance" meant to them. The survey resulted in an assortment of answers. The majority of those who participated in the survey stated that they believed the word "repentance" meant one or more of the following:

- To feel sorry about something one did or failed to do.

- To feel remorseful about some act and to ask for forgiveness for it.

- To walk forward in a church service to formally ask Jesus into one's life.

Before we go any further, let's include *you* in the survey. How would you define the meaning of the word "repent"? Try to answer that question before reading on.

The word "repent" is a very important New Testament word. The first instances where this word is used in the New Testament are in Matthew 3:2 and Matthew 4:17 by John the Baptist and Jesus, respectively. John the Baptist proclaimed, "...*Repent* ye: for the kingdom of heaven is at hand" (Matthew 3:2). John's ministry was literally launched with that one word "repent."

Jesus, too, began His public ministry by beckoning His listeners to repent. In Matthew 4:17, Jesus commenced His preaching ministry when He said, "...*Repent:* for the kingdom of heaven is at hand." Like John the Baptist, Jesus knew that the only way to enter the Kingdom of God was through repentance.

Then in Acts 2:38, Peter launched his preaching ministry with the same requirement of repentance. Just as John the Baptist and Jesus had called on men to repent, so Peter told his audience in Acts 2:38, "*Repent.*"

Peter understood that repentance is the "birth canal" through which people enter the Kingdom of God. In other words, it is the only way to truly be delivered from the kingdom of darkness and to emerge spiritually reborn and filled with the God-kind of life.

The word "repent" used by John the Baptist, Jesus, and Peter is the Greek word *metanoeo*. It is a compound of the words *meta* and *nous*. The word *meta* means *to turn*, and the word *nous* refers to *the mind*. When these two words are compounded, the new word describes in its most basic sense *a change of mind* or *a complete conversion*. The word *metanoeo* reflects *a turn*, *a change of direction*, *a new course*, and *a completely altered behavior and view of life.*

In the New Testament, this Greek word is used to denote *a complete, radical, total change.* It means *a decision to completely change one's thoughts, behavior, and actions* or *to entirely turn around in the way one is thinking, believing, or living.* Thus, the word "repent" in the New Testament gives the image of a person changing from top to bottom — a total transformation wholly affecting every part of a person's life.

I must point out the importance of the word *nous* contained in this definition of repentance.

As we have seen above, the word *nous* is the Greek word for *the mind.* This means that the decision to repent lies in the *mind, not* in the *emotions.* This is not the same as a fleeting sorrow for past actions; rather, it is a solid, intellectual decision *to turn about-face, take a new direction, and revise the pattern of one's life.*

Emotions may accompany repentance, but they are not required in order to repent. True repentance is *a mental choice to leave what is displeasing to God, and to turn toward Him with all of one's heart and mind in order to follow Jesus.*

A prime example of such a *turning* can be seen in Paul's first letter to the Thessalonian believers when he commended them for the way in which they had "…turned to God from idols to serve the living and true God" (1 Thessalonians 1:9). The word "turned" in this verse is the Greek word *epistrepho*, which means *to completely turn in a new direction.*

Paul said the Thessalonian believers turned from idols "to serve the living and true God." The word "serve" is important, for it tells us that the turn they made produced a life change with visible fruit that reflected the transformation. It is the word *douleuo*, the word for *a servant*, implying that the Thessalonian believers had fully left behind idolatry and had completely dedicated their lives to serving Jesus.

By using this word *douleuo*, Paul informed us that the Thessalonians didn't just claim to have repented; they showed it by changing the way they *thought* and *lived* and *served*. Their dramatically different outward behavior was *guaranteed proof* that real repentance had occurred.

The word "repent" — from the Greek word *metanoeo* — denotes *a change of mind* that has accompanying actions. Repentance is not the mere acceptance of a new philosophy or new idea. *It is a conversion to truth so deep that it results in a total life change.*

The idea of an across-the-board transformation is intrinsic to the word "repent." In fact, if there is no transformation, change of behavior, or change of desire in a person who claims to have repented, it is doubtful that true repentance ever occurred, no matter what the person claims. Real repentance begins with a decision to make an about-face and to change, but its *proof* can be witnessed as a person's outward conduct consistently complies with that decision.

We sing the old song, "Just as I Am, Without One Plea"[1] — and certainly we do come to God "just as we are." However, God doesn't expect us to *remain* the way we are. He expects change, and that is what repentance is all about.

As you will see in the pages to come, repentance is part of the lifestyle of a serious believer. We repent to begin our relationship with God, and as we grow in our walk with God, the Holy Spirit will continue to reveal things in our lives that need to change. When He opens our eyes to those things that are displeasing to Him, we must be willing to repent — to make an intelligent decision to adjust our thinking and behavior to conform to God's ways.

---

[1]Charlotte Elliott, "Just As I Am," *The Christian Remembrancer Pocket Book* (Poetry, 1835).

2

THE RIGHT KIND
OF PAIN

None of us likes pain. Yet pain is very important because it is a signal designed to alert us, for example, when something is wrong in our bodies. Our response to physical pain may be to determine the root of the problem or to simply numb the discomfort with painkillers. The painkillers may work for a while, but when the numbing effect wears off, the pain often reemerges because its source was never identified and corrected.

The only way to permanently get rid of pain is to go to the root of the problem. Once the source is identified and the correct treatment is applied, the pain can usually be eliminated.

We live in an age when people want to be told everything is going to be all right. But the truth is, some things are *not* going to be all right unless a change is made. We must love people enough to be honest with them, regardless of how painful it is for them to hear the truth.

It's good to preach uplifting messages. In fact, this is something we need to do in a world where there is so much hurt, depression, difficulties, and disappointments. Certainly we need to be a source of encouragement to church members and other people who feel put down by life.

But when non-Christians or Christians knowingly living in sin are in our midst, we are obligated to make sure they understand that sin separates them from God. They are *not* all right with God. It may be painful for them to hear the reality of their situation, but we must not merely toss "painkillers" at people who are lost or out of fellowship with the Lord to numb them and keep them ignorant of the truth. We must ask the Holy Spirit to help us open their eyes to the root of the problem in their lives — their spiritual condition.

When we're speaking about the subject of sin to the unsaved or to those who have strayed from their walk with the Lord, we must address the *root*. All the motivational and "how-to" sermons in the world cannot cure a sinful or wayward heart. Certainly we're to behave lovingly toward people who live sinful lives. But a person's sin cannot be changed by just a pat on the back or a hug around the neck!

In Acts 2:37 and 38, we see how God used the apostle Peter to address unbelievers on the Day of Pentecost.

Now when they heard this, they were pricked to their heart, and said unto Peter and to the rest of the apostles,

**Men and brethren, what shall we do?
Then Peter said unto them, *Repent*....**
                                    — Acts 2:37,38

With a no-nonsense, unapologetic, and dir-ect approach, Peter preached the Gospel with power. He didn't attack his listeners, and nei-ther should we attack those we are trying to reach. There is never a reason to attack or to speak disparagingly to people when sharing the Gospel. Even if people are dead in sin, they were made in the image of God — and Jesus died on the Cross for them. They deserve to be spoken to with dignity and respect.

Peter was respectful, yet he was forthright and honest as he went straight for the root of his listeners' problem. He preached a message that made them so extremely uncomfortable and inwardly pained that they cried out to learn how to be saved!

Acts 2:37 tells us the effect Peter's message had on his listeners: "Now when they [the

unsaved crowd] heard this, they were pricked
to their heart, and said unto Peter and to the
rest of the apostles, Men and brethren, what
shall we do?"

I want you to especially notice that this
verse says, "They were pricked to their heart."
The word "pricked" in this verse is the Greek
word *katanusso*, a word that means *to prick*, *to
puncture*, *to stab*, *to sting*, *to stun*, or *to pierce*.

The only other time the word *katanusso* is
found in the New Testament is in John 19:34
where John writes about Jesus: "But one of the
soldiers with a spear *pierced* his side, and forth-
with came there out blood and water." The
word "pierced" in this verse is from this same
root word *nusso*. It tells how the soldiers with a
spear *pierced*, *punctured*, *stabbed*, and *sliced open*
Jesus' side. It was a *deep puncturing* of His side
that pierced even His lungs.

This same root word is used in Acts 2:37,
where it is translated as "pricked" in the *King*

James Version. This tells us that Peter's words had the effect of *puncturing* their consciences, causing them to feel inwardly *sliced wide open* by his message, as we will see.

Peter's listeners were *deeply disturbed* when they heard his message. That message gave them such an intense *stab* to their hearts that it *penetrated* their conscience, *sliced open* their souls, *punctured* them in their inmost being, and *cut* them so deeply on the inside that they cried out for help. The message *stung* their hearts and minds as they became aware of their sin. Suddenly their souls felt an *ache*.

When Peter stood before that crowd and preached to them, he knew they needed truth that would change them, not a painkiller that would make them feel good while failing to remedy their very serious problem. The root of the problem had to be identified so it could be dealt with and eliminated.

For those unbelievers to have a change of nature, it would require repentance. To that end, Peter presented the truth boldly, plainly, and with no apologies.

That day the Holy Spirit reached deep into those people's hearts and convicted them of their sinful condition. The crowd wasn't offended by Peter's message. In fact, Acts 2:41 tells us that the unbelieving crowd "gladly received his word."

People are usually thankful when someone tells them the truth, even if it is painful to hear at first. They appreciate an honest approach. That day more than 3,000 souls came into the Kingdom of God as a result of a piercing produced in people's hearts by Peter's honest preaching of the Word. That was a very impressive outcome!

As we present truth to people who are non-Christians or to those who are wayward Christians, we don't need to be ugly or harsh.

But neither do we need to water down the truth or act apologetically regarding what the Bible teaches.

When truth is presented clearly and powerfully, it puts a sharp, doubled-edged sword into the hands of the Holy Spirit, which He uses to penetrate people's hearts. When the message is watered down, it dulls the edge of the blade and makes it more difficult for the Holy Spirit to slice through the demonic strongholds created in people's minds by sinful habits, bondages, and spiritual darkness.

Of course, we must always allow the Holy Spirit to lead us in knowing how and when to present the truth to someone who is unsaved or who has strayed away from the Lord. Then as we speak in a spirit of compassion — and as we do it boldly and straightforwardly — the root of the listener's problem will be identified so he or she can make the choice to repent and allow the Holy Spirit to eliminate it by His power.

We must never forget that the Gospel is the "power of God unto salvation" (*see* Romans 1:16). There is never a reason for us to be ashamed of the Gospel or to apologize for the requirements God has set forth for all who would come to Him.

When the unsaved crowd heard Peter preach that day, their hearts were sliced so wide open by the truth Peter preached that they cried out, "…Men and brethren, what shall we do?" (Acts 2:37). The people asked Peter and the other apostles to tell them what steps were required for them to be made right with God. That's when Peter boldly told them: *"Repent."*

And that's the pattern we're to follow as we share truth with the lost or with those who need to be restored in fellowship with the Lord. We must present the truth compellingly, compassionately, and clearly enough for them to understand the real root of their problem. We are not to comfort the lost and the backslidden so that we leave them feeling like they're all right in their sin; rather, we are called to help them understand their need to repent.

The truth is, people may at first feel stung by what we tell them, but that sting may be the very thing that brings them to the point of repentance. Sin and its consequences are eternal and unchangeable after death.

For the unsaved, the stakes couldn't be higher. A wrong choice results in eternal torment in hell, forever separated from the presence of God. For wayward Christians, they stand to lose much when they trade a life of obedience for sinful pleasure and willful disobedience. If we love these individuals, we will lovingly tell them the truth to help them come back into spiritual sobriety and get their spiritual priorities in right order again.

Think of people you know who need to receive Jesus as their Savior — as well as Christian who have strayed and who need to rededicate their lives to the Lord. Do you love them enough to sit down with them and tell them the truth, explaining how serious their spiritual condition is according to the Word of God? If you were unsaved — or living in a backslidden state — wouldn't you hope someone would care about *you* enough to tell you the truth?

3

WHAT IS GODLY SORROW?

A study of the New Testament makes it clear that repentance is a requirement for a non-Christian to come to God. It is also a vital part of the Christian walk for every committed believer.

True repentance is different than simply being "sorry" for doing wrong.

We see this distinction in the case of the Corinthian church. When Paul wrote his first letter to the Corinthians, he addressed many problems that existed in the congregation at Corinth, including strife, selfish ambition, and drunkenness. However, the most notorious problem was an act of immorality by a brother in the

29

church who was committing fornication with his father's wife (*see* 1 Corinthians 5:1).

Paul was so stunned by this act of immorality that he told the Corinthians that this kind of immorality didn't even exist among non-Christians. Paul loved this congregation, and he didn't want to see the church there jeopardized. Therefore, he adamantly urged these believers to take immediate action against these spiritually poisonous activities before the whole church became contaminated.

It is clear in reading Paul's second letter to the Corinthians that this congregation took Paul's orders very seriously. They must have been embarrassed and saddened by the fact that Paul had to rebuke them, because the apostle told them, "...I made you sorry with my letter..." (2 Corinthians 7:8 *NKJV*).

The word "sorry" is from the Greek word *lupeo*, which describes *pain* or *grief*. Apparently Paul's first letter caused the Corinthian

congregation to feel deeply *pained* and *grieved*.
Paul knew this had been their response so he
went on to tell them, "...I perceive that the
same epistle made you sorry...." Twice in Second Corinthians 7:8, Paul acknowledged that
they had been pained by the previous letter he
sent them.

However, Paul continued in Second Corinthians 7:9 (*NKJV*) by saying, "Now I rejoice,
not that you were made sorry, but that your
sorrow led to repentance. For you were made
sorry in a godly manner...."

The word "sorrowed" is again from the
Greek word *lupeo*, denoting *pain* or *grief*. The
word "repentance" is *metanoeo*, which refers to
a complete, radical, total change. As we saw previously, it is *a decision to completely change or to
entirely turn around in the way one is thinking,
believing, or living.*

Paul revealed that the Corinthians didn't
just listen to his earlier message — they heeded

31

it completely and made the decision to *change*. In fact, they had obeyed him so entirely that they experienced a total transformation, making them unrecognizable from the sinful condition for which Paul rebuked them in a previous epistle. Thus, the entire phrase in Second Corinthians 7:9 could be interpreted, *"I don't rejoice that I caused you to feel pain and grief, but I do rejoice that my letter made you purpose in your hearts to change...."*

Paul went on to elaborate: "...For you were made sorry in a godly manner...." This phrase "godly manner" could be translated as, *"Your pain was in response to God's dealing with you."* The Holy Spirit had used Paul's earlier epistle to prick their hearts, and Paul was quick to acknowledge this.

Although the sorrow that the Corinthian believers felt may have been initiated by Paul's letter, the truth was that their hearts felt pained because *God's Spirit* was dealing with them. Thus, the verse could be rendered, *"I don't rejoice that I caused you to feel pain and grief, but I rejoice that my letter made you want to change. Your pain was your response to God's dealing with you...."*

The Corinthian Christians were prompt to respond to God's dealings with them. In fact, they acted so swiftly and seriously to obey Paul's instruction that in his next letter to them, the apostle declared, "For observe this very thing, that you sorrowed in a godly manner: What diligence it produced in you, what clearing of yourselves, what indignation, what fear, what vehement desire, what zeal, what vindication! In all things you proved yourselves to be clear in this matter" (v. 11 *NKJV*).

Not wanting to grieve the Holy Spirit any longer, the Christians in Corinth moved with urgency to repent and purge themselves of sin and carnality. Their actions were *outward proof* that genuine repentance had occurred.

As we have seen, true repentance produces an indisputable transformation in one's behavior. The change in the Corinthian church was evidence enough for Paul to say they were now completely "clear" in the matters where they had previously been wrong. They had been completely exonerated!

Have you ever felt sorrow because of a sin you committed that grieved the heart of God? Did you allow that godly sorrow to do its full work in you and produce a desire to change within your heart — resulting in a change in your character, behavior, and lifestyle? Or did you merely brush off that sorrow and thereby resist God's dealings with you *and* His grace to help you grow?

If we will be sensitive to the Holy Spirit and listen to His voice, we will hear Him speak to us when we do something that grieves the heart of God. In that moment, we have a choice: We can harden our hearts and turn a deaf ear to God's Spirit, or we can allow the Holy Spirit to deal deeply with us and produce a desire in us to *never* transgress in that particular way again.

God is willing to work in us and with us, but we must have hearts that want to positively respond to His dealings.

Take some time to evaluate how God's Spirit has been trying to deal with you. Can you honestly say that you've allowed a godly sorrow to have its full effect in you — thereby producing a strong desire to change and never fail in the same way again? Regardless of what you have done, God offers you forgiveness, and He will give you the strength needed to enact powerful, permanent change in your life if your heart is truly repentant. *It's up to you.*

4

THE DIFFERENCE BETWEEN REMORSE, GUILT, REGRET, AND REPENTANCE

I remember an experience as a young boy growing up in church that made a huge impact on my life and helped me understand the vast difference between two words: *remorse* and true *repentance*. Each year we had revival meetings in our church. It was at one of these revival meetings that I heard an evangelist preach about hell, and I became so convicted of sin that I committed my life to Jesus.

However, not long after I walked the aisle and received Christ, I began to seriously doubt whether I had really been saved. This doubt stemmed from watching what happened when others got saved, which was entirely different from my own experience.

Adults often wept and wept when they bowed at the altar, but I didn't shed a tear the day I got saved. The devil began to torment me every day with thoughts, such as: *Why didn't you cry when you went forward to give your heart to Christ? Maybe you're not really saved! If you were really sincere, shouldn't you have cried like all the others did when they repented and got saved?*

But growing up in church gives a person time to watch people and learn, and as time passed, I began to notice a very important trend. Frequently the people who cried buckets of tears at the altar during revival meetings were the same people who came forward in the altar calls every year!

38

I also noticed that after these "criers" walked out the door of the church, many of them didn't show their faces in church again until the next year's revival meeting. Then once again, they ended up back on their knees at the altar — once again crying buckets of tears.

Finally, it dawned on me what was happening. Many of those who repeatedly came forward to weep profusely at the altar never changed. Although they used nearly an entire box of tissues sobbing, it appeared that nothing much deeper occurred than the shedding of tears. I began to realize that a show of emotion isn't always a sign of repentance; sometimes it's only evidence of *remorse.*

Real repentance is very different from remorse.

Repentance produces true *change*, whereas remorse merely produces natural *sorrow*, which is often confused with repentance. But there is an enormous difference between repentance and remorse.

A perfect New Testament example of remorse is found in Matthew 27:3-5, where the Bible tells us about Judas Iscariot after his betrayal of Jesus. It says, "Then Judas, which had betrayed him, when he saw that he was condemned, repented himself, and brought again the thirty pieces of silver to the chief priests and elders, saying, I have sinned in that I have betrayed the innocent blood. And they said, What is that to us? See thou to that. And he cast down the pieces of silver in the temple, and departed, and went and hanged himself."

Notice the Bible says that Judas "repented" himself. Usually a person who repents doesn't go out and hang himself afterward, so what really happened in this passage? The answer lies in the word "repented" that is used in verse 3.

This is not the word *metanoeo*, the word most often used that means "repent" in the

New Testament. Instead, this particular word for "repent" is the Greek word *metamelomai*, which portrays a person who is completely overwhelmed with emotions. This word is used five times in the New Testament, and in each instance, it expresses *sorrow*, *mourning*, or *grief*. The word *metamelomai* rarely gives the picture of someone moved to change, but rather depicts a person who is seized with *remorse*, *guilt*, or *regret*.

- *Metamelomai* can depict *remorse* that grips a person because of an act he committed that he knows is wrong. If he were willing to repent, he could be forgiven and could change. But because he has no plans to repent, stop his sinful activities, and try to rectify what he has done, he is therefore gripped with *remorse*. Consequently, this emotion produces *no change* — no repentance — in a person's life.

41

- *Metamelomai* can also express the *guilt* a person feels because he knows that he *has done wrong*, that he *will continue to do wrong*, and that he *has no plans to change* his course of action. He feels shameful about what he is doing but continues to do it anyway, which results in a state of ongoing guilt. This guilt produces *no change* in a person's life or behavior. Yet genuine repentance would fix this feeling of guilt and remove it completely.

- *Metamelomai* best denotes the *regret* a person feels because he is *caught* doing something wrong. He isn't repentant for committing the sin; instead, he is sorrowful only because he *got caught*. Now he's in trouble. Rather than being repentant, this person is *regretful* that he got caught and must now pay the consequences. Chances are that if he'd never been caught, he would have continued his activities. This kind of regret likewise produces *no change* in a person's heart, conduct, or life.

Because the word *metamelomai* is used in Matthew 27:3, it means Judas Iscariot did not "repent" in the sense that he was sorry for what he did and wanted to make it right with God. Rather, he was *remorseful*, seized with *guilt*, and filled with *regret*. Because of his actions, Judas knew he had blown his opportunity to be a high-ranking member of Jesus' inner circle. *Judas was more sorrowful for himself than he was for his participation in Jesus' betrayal.*

Don't misunderstand me — emotion and tears *may* accompany repentance. If we have sinned against the Holy Spirit, it is normal for us to experience godly sorrow for our actions.

But godly sorrow produces more than tears; it produces a desire to change that leads us to deliverance, freedom, and salvation in the fullest sense of the word. *What a contrast to the sorrow of the world that produces hopelessness, defeat, and despair.*

When I was a child and Satan tormented me because I didn't cry at the altar when I got saved, I *was* indeed saved. I just had no tears to cry over my horrid sins *because I was five years old when I committed my life to Christ*!

Even though I didn't cry, my *decision* to serve Jesus was firm and therefore absolutely real. As a result of this experience, I learned to not confuse sobbing with repentance.

Tears and emotions may accompany the decision to repent, but they're not requirements, nor are they necessarily evidence that repentance has occurred.

Remember, the word translated "repent" is *metanoeo* — referring to *a complete turn in the way one thinks, lives, or acts.* For a person to repent, he must simply make up his mind *to change.* God will help, but the decision to change starts with the person.

So what is the difference between guilt, remorse, regret, and repentance?

- *Guilt* is a prison that will keep you perpetually bound and *unchanged*.

- *Remorse* enslaves you in sorrow that engulfs you emotionally and leaves you feeling sad, depressed, hopeless, and *unchanged*.

- *Regret* is self-pity that is focused more on your own personal loss than on the pain or loss you caused to others or to the heart of God, and it leaves you *unchanged*.

- *Repentance* is a heartfelt, quality decision *to change*. And when genuine repentance occurs in a person's heart and mind, you can be sure the Holy Spirit will release His power to effect change in that person's life and lead him to *freedom*!

I encourage you to set aside time to commune with the Holy Spirit about these very personal matters. Give Him permission to take you on a tour behind the doors of each "room" of your life. Let Him help you see what you need to see in order to grow into all God has created you to be.

Are there any areas in your life in which you have felt guilty, remorseful, or regretful — but unchanged? Could it be that you've never really made a firm decision to change, and that's why you've had no enduring victory in those areas of your life?

If you've confused tears with repentance, now you know that you don't have to depend on your emotions to repent. If God is dealing with you about something that needs to change in your life, you can repent right now at this very moment, regardless of what you do or do not feel.

5

REPENTANCE — AN ELEMENTARY PRINCIPLE

It's amazing to realize that many Christians today don't understand the spiritual truths we just discussed in the last four chapters.

What would you think of a full-grown adult who never got serious about learning his ABCs and therefore had to keep repeating the first grade over and over again? Imagine that 50 or so years have passed since that person first entered grade school. As he nears his sixtieth birthday, there he still sits at a tiny little desk in a room full of young first-graders.

Would you find that to be a normal situation?

Strange as that scenario may seem, it happens all the time in the Christian community. Many believers who have known the Lord for years have remained at the level of spiritual immaturity they were at as baby Christians. They never applied themselves or got serious about their spiritual growth; thus, they perpetually remain spiritually immature.

Although these Christians have been saved for many years, they are still sitting in "beginners' class" in Sunday school with children, figuratively speaking. They should be much further along in their spiritual growth, but because they were never diligent about their walk with God, they just keep repeating the basics over and over again.

In Hebrews 6:1 and 2, the writer of Hebrews listed what is referred to as "the principles of the doctrines of Christ."

Therefore leaving the principles of the doctrine of Christ, let us go on unto perfection; not laying again the foundation of repentance from dead works, and of faith toward God, of the doctrine of baptisms, and of laying on of hands, and of resurrection of the dead, and of eternal judgment.

The word "principles" is the Greek word *arches*, which denotes something that is *original, early,* or *from the beginning*. In Hebrews 6:1, this word *arches* specifically refers to the *elementary principles* of Christ.

These elementary principles comprise the fundamental doctrine for *beginners*. They encompass the basic spiritual principles that every new believer should know, as well as the first steps of faith that every baby Christian should be able to take. In other words, these are the *ABCs of the Christian faith*!

The problem is, many Christians aren't very familiar with these elementary principles.

In fact, some don't even know them at all. This failure to know the fundamental truths of the Christian faith causes them to struggle in life. Had they been taught and then applied themselves at an earlier age, they would be much further along in their walk with God and therefore able to overcome the difficulties that confront them in life. But because they never took time to learn the basics, they are still sitting in a spiritual "beginners' class"!

In the list of vital elementary principles found in Hebrews 6, the very first one mentioned is "...the foundation of repentance from dead works..." (v. 1).

This word "foundation" is the Greek word *themelios*. It is a combination of the Greek word *lithos*, which means *stone*, and the word *tithemi*, which means *to place*. When these words are combined, the new compound word denotes *something that is set in stone; a foundation that cannot be easily moved or shaken;* or *something so solid that it will endure the test of time.* Taken

50

together, these different nuances of meaning are the reason the word *themelios* came to be translated as the word "foundation."

By using the Greek word *themelios*, the writer of Hebrews was teaching us that if we are serious about our walk with God, our understanding of repentance will be positioned as a spiritual foundation that is *set in stone*. This principle of repentance should be so rock-solid in our lives that we are *immovable* and *unshakable* on this subject.

However, this is sadly not the case for many believers in the modern Church. We saw earlier that many churchgoing Christians who were surveyed couldn't even provide an accurate definition of the word "repent"!

This is very alarming because it reveals that most believers are in a stunted state of spiritual maturity. Regardless of their age or how many years they've been saved, multitudes of people are still in "beginners' class." If they still can't articulate an answer to such a simple question, *they are still in spiritual kindergarten!*

Hebrews 6:1 states that our knowledge concerning repentance should be so set in stone that it should never have to be repeated or taught to us again. It reads, "...*not laying again* the foundation of repentance from dead works...."

The words "not laying again" are derived from a Greek word that means *to lay something down*. The use of this word in Hebrews 6:1 tells us that the elementary principles of the Christian faith should be laid down in our lives like a strong foundation as soon as we come to Christ. And once this foundation is set in place, there should *never* be any need for it to be laid down again.

In fact, Hebrews 6:1 says that seasoned Christians should be able to leave the fundamental truths behind and "go on unto perfection." The word "leaving" in this verse is from the Greek word *aphiemi*, which means *to leave it* or *to let it go*. It does not refer to the abandonment of truth, but rather the realization that maturity requires pressing upward to the next level.

In other words, the beginning is not a stopping point — it is only a beginning!

This is why the writer of Hebrews continued by saying we must "go on unto perfection...."

The words "go on" are derived from the word *phero*, which means *to carry* or *to bear*. However, the tense used in this verse paints the picture of *a force that carries one onward* or *a force that bears one further*. It could literally be translated *let us be carried*, and it conveys the idea that as we grow spiritually, the Holy Spirit picks us up and personally carries us forward in our knowledge and understanding of God.

But where is the Holy Spirit carrying us? Hebrews 6:1 tells us that He is carrying us toward "perfection." The word "perfection" is the Greek word *teleiotes*, which refers to *a child graduating from one class to the next until he finally reaches maturity.*

This means that until we meet Jesus face to face in Heaven, there is no end to our spiritual growth. That's why it is so very serious when an older Christian who has been saved for many years can't even articulate the meaning of the word "repentance." He should be much further along in his spiritual growth, but instead of reaching maturity, he is stuck in spiritual kindergarten.

Why is it so essential and elementary that we know and understand the doctrine of repentance?

As we discussed in Chapter One, the word "repentance" in the New Testament depicts *a complete, radical, total change.* It is *a decision to completely change* or *a decision to entirely turn around in the way that one is thinking, believing, and living.* It describes a person who is undergoing a complete and radical transformation that literally affects every part of his or her life.

54

We've seen that repentance is not a fleeting, temporary sorrow for past actions. Rather, it is a solid, intellectual decision to turn around and take a new direction in order to completely change the patterns of one's life on every level. It is a mental choice to turn toward God with all of one's heart in order to follow Jesus completely.

Repentance is the starting place for everyone and a lifestyle for every committed Christian. As Christians who are serious about their walk with God, we must be willing to quickly repent every time we have done something out of character as those who represent Jesus.

This is a basic, foundational act of the Christian life. It is our starting place, and it is a part of the committed Christian's lifestyle. It is the place where our turning away from sin begins, and it is the point from which we submit, and *continually submit*, our lives to the lordship of Jesus Christ.

So let the truths contained within these pages help you make sure that your understanding of this essential "elementary doctrine" is laid down like a strong, immovable foundation in your life. Once you are well established in a life of continual repentance and submission before the Lord, the Holy Spirit will carry you onward and upward as you reach toward spiritual maturity.

The fullness of God's great plan for your life lies on the road ahead!

PRAYER OF SALVATION

When Jesus Christ comes into your life, you are immediately emancipated — totally set free from the bondage of sin! If you have never received Jesus as your personal Savior, it is time to experience this new life for yourself. The first step to freedom is simple. Just pray this prayer from your heart:

Lord, I can never adequately thank You for all You did for me on the Cross. I am so undeserving, Jesus, but You came and gave Your life for me anyway. I repent for rejecting You, and I turn away from my life of rebellion and sin right now. I turn to You and receive You as my Savior, and I ask You to wash away my sin and make me completely new in You by Your precious blood. I thank You from the depths of my heart for doing what no

57

*one else could do for me. Had it not been
for Your willingness to lay down Your life
for me, I would be eternally lost.*

*Thank You, Jesus, that I am now redeemed
by Your blood. On the Cross, You bore
my sin, my sickness, my pain, my lack of
peace, and my suffering. Your blood has
removed my sin, washed me whiter than
snow, and given me rightstanding with
the Father. I have no need to be ashamed
of my past sins because I am now a new
creature in You. Old things have passed
away, and all things have become new
because I am in Jesus Christ (2 Corinthians 5:17).*

*Because of You, Jesus, today I am for-
given; I am filled with peace; and I am a
joint-heir with You! Satan no longer has
a right to lay any claim on me. From a
grateful heart, I will faithfully serve You
the rest of my days!*

If you prayed this prayer from your heart, something amazing has happened to you. No longer a servant to sin, you are now a servant of Almighty God. The evil spirits that once exacted every ounce of your being and required your all-inclusive servitude no longer possess the authorization to control you or dictate your destiny!

As a result of your decision to turn your life over to Jesus Christ, your eternal home has been decided forever. Heaven will now be your permanent address for all eternity.

God's Spirit has moved into your own human spirit, and you have become the "temple of God" (1 Corinthians 6:19). What a miracle! To think that God, by His Spirit, now lives inside you!

Now you have a new Lord and Master, and His name is Jesus. From this moment on, the Spirit of God will work in you and supernaturally energize you to fulfill God's will for your life.

Everything will change for you as you yield to His leadership in your life — and it's all going to change for the best!

SCRIPTURES ON REPENTANCE FOR PRAYER

If my people, who are called by my name, will humble themselves and pray and seek my face and turn from their wicked ways, then I will hear from heaven, and I will forgive their sin and will heal their land (2 Chronicles 7:14 *NIV*).

Rend your heart and not your garments. Return to the Lord your God, for he is gracious and compassionate, slow to anger and abounding in love, and he relents from sending calamity (Joel 2:13 *NIV*).

…"Return to me," declares the Lord Almighty, "and I will return to you," says the Lord Almighty (Zechariah 1:3 *NIV*).

Whoever conceals their sins does not prosper, but the one who confesses and renounces them finds mercy (Proverbs 28:13 *NIV*).

Produce fruit in keeping with repentance (Matthew 3:8 *NIV*).

From that time on Jesus began to preach, "Repent, for the kingdom of heaven has come near" (Matthew 4:17 *NIV*).

Repent, then, and turn to God, so that your sins may be wiped out, that times of refreshing may come from the Lord (Acts 3:19 *NIV*).

Truly, these times of ignorance God overlooked, but now commands all men everywhere to repent (Acts 17:30 *NKJV*).

The Lord is not slow in keeping his promise, as some understand slowness. Instead he is patient with you, not wanting anyone to perish, but everyone to come to repentance (2 Peter 3:9 *NIV*).

If we confess our sins, he is faithful and just and will forgive us our sins and purify us from all unrighteousness (1 John 1:9 *NIV*).

Come near to God and he will come near to you. Wash your hands, you sinners, and purify your hearts, you double-minded (James 4:8 *NIV*).

…You have persevered and have patience, and have labored for My name's sake and have not become weary. Nevertheless I have this against you, that you have left your first love. Remember therefore from where you have fallen; repent and do the first works, or else I will come to you quickly and remove your lampstand from its place — unless you repent (Revelation 2:3-5 *NKJV*).

REFERENCE BOOK LIST

1. *How To Use New Testament Greek Study Aids* by Walter Jerry Clark (Loizeaux Brothers).

2. *Strong's Exhaustive Concordance of the Bible* by James H. Strong.

3. *The Interlinear Greek-English New Testament* by George Ricker Berry (Baker Book House).

4. *The Englishman's Greek Concordance of the New Testament* by George Wigram (Hendrickson).

5. *New Thayer's Greek-English Lexicon of the New Testament* by Joseph Thayer (Hendrickson).

6. *The Expanded Vine's Expository Dictionary of New Testament Words* by W. E. Vine (Bethany).

7. *New International Dictionary of New Testament Theology* (*DNTT*); Colin Brown, editor (Zondervan).

8. *Theological Dictionary of the New Testament* (*TDNT*) by Geoffrey Bromiley; Gephard Kittle, editor (Eerdmans Publishing Co.).

9. *The New Analytical Greek Lexicon*; Wesley Perschbacher, editor (Hendrickson).

10. *The Linguistic Key to the Greek New Testament* by Fritz Rienecker and Cleon Rogers (Zondervan).

11. *Word Studies in the Greek New Testament* by Kenneth Wuest, 4 Volumes (Eerdmans).

12. *New Testament Words* by William Barclay (Westminster Press).

ABOUT THE AUTHOR

 **Rick Renner** is a prolific author and a highly respected Bible teacher and leader in the international Christian community. Rick is the author of more than 30 books, including the best-sellers *Dressed To Kill* and *Sparkling Gems From the Greek 1*, which have sold more than 3 million copies combined.

In 1991, Rick and his family moved to what is now the former Soviet Union. Today he is the senior pastor of the Moscow Good News Church and the founder of Media Mir, the first Christian television network in the former USSR that today broadcasts the Gospel to countless Russian-speaking viewers around the world via multiple satellites and the Internet.

He is also the founder and president of Rick Renner Ministries, based in Tulsa, Oklahoma, and host to his TV program that is seen around the world. Rick's wife and lifelong ministry partner, Denise, along with their three sons — Paul, Philip, and Joel — and their families, lead this amazing work with the help of their committed leadership team.

CONTACT RENNER MINISTRIES

For further information
about RENNER Ministries, please contact
the RENNER Ministries office nearest you,
or visit the ministry website at **www.renner.org**.

**ALL USA
CORRESPONDENCE:**
RENNER Ministries
P. O. Box 702040
Tulsa, OK 74170-2040
(918) 496-3213
or 1-800-RICK-593
Email: renner@renner.org
Website: www.renner.org

MOSCOW OFFICE:
RENNER Ministries
P. O. Box 789
101000, Russia, Moscow
+7 (495) 727-14-67
Email: partner@rickrenner.ru
Website: www.ignc.org

RIGA OFFICE:

RENNER Ministries
Unijas 99
Riga LV-1084, Latvia
+371 67802150
Email: info@goodnews.lv

KIEV OFFICE:

RENNER Ministries
P. O. Box 300
01001, Ukraine, Kiev
+38 (044) 451-8115
Email: partner@rickrenner.ru

OXFORD OFFICE:

RENNER Ministries
Box 7, 266 Banbury Road
Oxford OX2 7DL, England 44
+44 (0) 1865 355509
Email: europe@renner.org

THE HARRISON HOUSE VISION

Proclaiming the truth and the power

of the Gospel of Jesus Christ with excellence.

Challenging Christians

to live victoriously,

grow spiritually,

know God intimately.

Harrison House

For all the latest Harrison House product
information,
including new releases,
email subscriptions,
testimonies, and monthly specials,
please visit **harrisonhouse.com**.

Notes

_____

_____

_____

_____

_____

_____

_____

_____

_____

_____

_____

_____

_____

_____

_____

_____

Notes

Notes

Notes

_____

_____

_____

_____

_____

_____

_____

_____

_____

_____

_____

_____

_____

_____

_____

_____

Notes

_____

_____

_____

_____

_____

_____

_____

_____

_____

_____

_____

_____

_____

_____

_____

Notes

_____

_____

_____

_____

_____

_____

_____

_____

_____

_____

_____

_____

_____

_____

Notes

Printed in Great Britain
by Amazon